marijuana today

The Benefits of
Medical Marijuana:
from Cancer to PTSD

marijuana today

The Benefits of Medical Marijuana:
from Cancer to PTSD

Growing Career Opportunities
in the Marijuana Industry

Marijuana: Facts, Figures, & Opinions

Marijuana in Society

Marijuana's Harmful Effects on Youth

marijuana today

The Benefits of
Medical Marijuana:
from Cancer to PTSD

Leigh Clayborne

MASON CREST

Mason Crest
450 Parkway Drive, Suite D
Broomall, Pennsylvania 19008
(866) MCP-BOOK (toll-free)
www.masoncrest.com

First printing
9 8 7 6 5 4 3 2 1

978-1-4222-4108-0 (hardback)
978-1-4222-4103-5 (series)
978-1-4222-7696-9 (ebook)

Cataloging-in-Publication Data on file with the Library of Congress

NATIONAL HIGHLIGHTS

Developed and Produced by National Highlights Inc.
Editor: Andrew Morkes
Interior and cover design: Yolanda Van Cooten
Proofreader: Mika Jin
Production: Michelle Luke

QR CODES AND LINKS TO THIRD-PARTY CONTENT

contents

Introduction 6

Chapter 1   What is Medical Marijuana? 9

Chapter 2   Medical Marijuana Use and Research
             Around the World...21

Chapter 3   Medical Marijuana and Mental Health 33

Chapter 4   Medical Marijuana and Physical Health 47

Chapter 5   The Future of Medical Marijuana 61

Series Glossary of Key Terms 72

Index 75

Further Reading & Internet Resources...............................79

KEY ICONS TO LOOK FOR:

Words to understand: These words with their easy-to-understand definitions will increase the reader's understanding of the text while building vocabulary skills.

Sidebars: This boxed material within the main text allows readers to build knowledge, gain insights, explore possibilities, and broaden their perspectives by weaving together additional information to provide realistic and holistic perspectives.

Educational Videos: Readers can view videos by scanning our QR codes, providing them with additional educational content to supplement the text. Examples include news coverage, moments in history, speeches, iconic sports moments and much more!

Text-dependent questions: These questions send the reader back to the text for more careful attention to the evidence presented there.

Research projects: Readers are pointed toward areas of further inquiry connected to each chapter. Suggestions are provided for projects that encourage deeper research and analysis.

Series glossary of key terms: This back-of-the-book glossary contains terminology used throughout this series. Words found here increase the reader's ability to read and comprehend higher-level books and articles in this field.

Introduction

There's nothing new about medical marijuana. As far as we know, it's been recognized for its medicinal properties since 2900 B.C. In ancient writings, the Chinese Emperor Fu Hsi noted its popularity. He called it a powerful medicine. The Chinese believed that marijuana possessed both yin and yang. In ancient Chinese medicine, these two properties were thought to bring wellness of mind and body when properly balanced. The ancient Egyptians used the pollen of the cannabis (marijuana) flower to treat many diseases. They treated everything from glaucoma (an eye disease) to inflammation. They were so fond of it, in fact, that archaeologists found it buried with the mummy of Pharaoh Ramses II. Around 1000 BC, the people of India began making a drink out of cannabis and milk to use as a mild anesthetic and cure-all. But not until very recently has modern science begun to recognize and research the potential health benefits of this plant.

Today, some believe that medical marijuana could be the answer for many people who are suffering from terrible diseases. Others see cannabis as a dangerous drug. To them, it's not unlike heroin or inappropriately-used painkillers such as oxycodone.

You may have your own beliefs about medical marijuana. You may have heard about it from friends, on TV, or on the internet. But what do you really know about this drug? Is it medicine? Is it a dangerous drug? Should medical marijuana be legal? We won't answer these questions for you. Instead, you'll use your own brain and you'll decide. In this book, we'll explore the research and debate around medical cannabis. We'll look at the studies together and separate some of the myths from what science has actually found. You'll begin by looking at what medical marijuana is. You'll delve into how it's used and what people hope to achieve by using it. You'll also look at some side effects and drawbacks that make some hesitant to see it as a beneficial, or helpful, drug. You'll explore how people use marijuana around the world. You'll check out the various laws in place in different countries like Canada and The Netherlands. You'll learn about countries such as Israel that are leading the way in research. You'll discover how medical marijuana may help people with anxiety, depression, seizures, and even cancer. You'll find out what the science really shows and what needs further research. Finally, we'll consider together what the future of medical marijuana might look like. Where might the research take us? Do we anticipate more or fewer countries legalizing marijuana for medicinal purposes?

What will you discover about marijuana that you didn't know? What current beliefs might you be able to back up with science after reading this book? Will this book change your mind? It's all up to you.

Let's take a look!

Cannabis oil extract is often used to treat children who have epileptic seizures.

words to understand

cannabis: The plant that marijuana comes from.

cannabidiol oil: A form of medicinal marijuana in which the THC may have been removed.

Schedule I drug: The highest classification of controlled substances in the United States. This usually means that the drug is illegal. It suggests that a drug has no medicinal benefits.

tetrahydrocannabinol (THC): The psychoactive chemical found in marijuana. Psychoactive means that it has the potential to alter people's mental state. This altered mental state can cause mental impairment.

chapter 1

What is Medical Marijuana?

Medical marijuana is a plant-based substance that can be recommended by doctors in some countries. Patients use it to treat and relieve:

- Nausea
- Pain
- Sleep problems
- Seizures
- And more

Many studies from around the world support its medicinal properties. As interest in the therapeutic (helpful in treating mental and physical health) effects of medical marijuana increases, the number of studies demonstrating its medicinal benefits increase. Some countries embrace medical marijuana for its therapeutic uses. Others consider any form of

The cannabis plant contains powerful antioxidants, which offer health benefits that are similar to those found in berries.

marijuana to be a dangerous drug. Like so many things in life, the truth lies somewhere in between. It can be therapeutic. But it also can have dangerous side effects. We'll look at both in this book.

Did You Know?

It is legal to cultivate, or grow, hemp cannabis in some U.S. states because it only has around .3 percent THC. It can be prepared in such a way that the THC is greatly reduced or not present.

Is Medical Marijuana Legal?

As of the writing of this book, marijuana is considered illegal by the federal government of the United States. It's a **Schedule I drug**, which means that it's very closely regulated like cocaine or heroin. It is legal in other countries such as Uruguay. For comparison, Schedule II drugs are prescription drugs like Ritalin and Oxycodone. Doctors may prescribe these drugs. But they may be abused. Because of this, doctors, pharmacies, and patients must work together to avoid letting them get into the hands of someone who wasn't prescribed them.

Marijuana is technically against the law nationally. However, some states have passed laws to make medical marijuana legal in their state. In a growing trend over the past decade, approximately thirty states in the U.S. have legalized medical marijuana to treat some conditions, and eight states have approved it for non-medicinal use (also known as recreational use).

This trend isn't just impacting the U.S. It's a global trend. Canada, Uruguay, Denmark, and Israel, for example, have already made medical marijuana legal in some way. Other countries continue to review the research to decide if it's right for them.

The Food and Drug Administration (FDA) is the U.S. agency responsible that regulates the safety and usage of food and medicine to treat medical conditions. It closely regulates all claims regarding the health benefits of substances like marijuana. Because the FDA hasn't approved medical marijuana for the treatment of any diseases, doctors in the U.S. cannot prescribe it. They can only recommend it in states where it's legal. Laws vary depending on the country or even the city you're in.

How Is Medical Marijuana Made and Used?

According to the Mayo Clinic, "medical marijuana is made from the dried leaves and buds of the **cannabis** sativa plant." Once the marijuana has been dried it can be used in several ways. It can be:

- Smoked
- Inhaled through a vaporizer
- Eaten in a food
- Drunk in tea or another beverage

Medical marijuana can also be put in creams and applied to the skin. And more recently, various companies have begun to make pills and drops that contain either substances found in marijuana or the whole plant.

The Anatomy of Medical Marijuana

When you think of marijuana, you may think about people "getting high" or "getting stoned." But medical marijuana actually has two key chemicals that have been shown to have medicinal effects. These substances are called cannabinoids. Each of them reacts with receptors in your body to produce a certain effect. Only one of them creates mental effects. The two main substances are called:

- Cannabidiol (CBD)
- **Tetrahydrocannabinol (THC)**

Medical marijuana became legal in Canada in 2001.

These substances undoubtedly work together when someone consumes marijuana. But studies also show that they can provide benefits when they are separated from the rest of the plant and used independently.

Learn more about CBD and THC.

Changing with the Times

Approximately 38 percent of high school seniors admit that they've tried marijuana, according to the National Institute on Drug Abuse. Perceptions about marijuana are changing around the world, but there are still risks you need to know about.

THC

THC is the psychoactive substance found in marijuana. Psychoactive means that it can cause unwanted mental effects. These vary among people and include:

- Inability to concentrate
- Slow reaction time
- Forgetfulness
- Drowsiness

Tetrahydrocannabinol, one of the main compounds in cannabis, has been found to reduce the severity of depression.

- Hunger
- Paranoia—extreme fear of something imagined

We'll talk more about side effects a little later. But as we'll look at in this book, THC may also:

- Reduce inflammation
- Control seizures
- Lessen depression symptoms
- And more

CBD

CBD is the second most common substance that makes up marijuana. By itself, it doesn't have negative mental effects like THC. Studies have shown that CBD can help:

- Reduce inflammation
- Reduce anxiety
- Reduce pain
- Control seizures
- Protect the nerves
- Help people relax

Some Marijuana Doesn't Get People High

CBD is a chemical found in the cannabis plant (marijuana). Studies have shown that it has many medicinal effects. Cannabis plants can be grown to have more CBD, and less THC. THC is the substance that has the mental effects. Children and teens who need medical marijuana usually use CBD for this reason.

It's also a powerful antioxidant. You can find antioxidants in many foods like berries, soybeans, grape juice, and chocolate. Antioxidants protect your body against harmful substances that you may come in contact with. Because of this, many believe they reduce your risk of cancer and many other diseases. Because CBD doesn't have mental effects, it's used to make medicines in some countries. CBD is the major ingredient in the prescription drug Sativex, an oral spray that is used to treat symptoms in patients with moderate to severe spasticity due to multiple sclerosis. Spasticity is a medical condition in which certain muscles are continuously contracted. Marijuana also contains many other substances that are less concentrated and have been less studied.

People commonly sell CBD as an oil. **Cannabidiol oil** can be made from hemp cannabis. In places where medical marijuana isn't legal, CBD oil may be legal. It's often used to treat children who have epileptic seizures. Those who suffer from epilepsy have difficulty doing normal things like playing sports, riding in a boat, or driving when they're older. They always must be careful. One study reported in the *Washington Post* found that children diagnosed with epilepsy who received CBD oil had 39 percent fewer seizures. These results give parents great hope and options for treating this horrible condition.

Let's briefly look at some of the promising aspects of using medical marijuana.

The Promising Aspects of Medical Marijuana

Researchers and advocates of medical marijuana are excited about the potential for what some consider a "miracle drug." In this book, we're going to take an in-depth look at some of the studies. But as an overview of what's to come, here are some of the findings that excite people who strongly support the use of medical marijuana.

- Medical marijuana can reduce the symptoms of post-traumatic stress disorder by 75 percent. (*Journal of Psychoactive Drugs*)

- Giving rats medical marijuana could help reduce stress during high-stress situations. (University of Buffalo, Research Institute on Addictions)
- People who take medical marijuana instead of prescription painkillers have been shown to be 50 percent less likely to suffer from anxiety and depression. (*Journal of Affective Disorders*)
- Medical marijuana may reduce the number of deaths from addiction to painkillers. (*JAMA Internal Medicine*)
- Medical marijuana was able to cut the number of muscle spasms in people with multiple sclerosis by one-third. (University of California, San Diego School of Medicine)

And the list goes on. We'll talk more about these in chapters three and four.

Find out how countries like Australia are studying the benefits of medical marijuana on people who have cancer.

The Risks of Taking Medical Marijuana

All medicines have some side effects. Just because medical marijuana comes from a plant, it doesn't mean that it's always 100 percent safe. The side effects are more severe in some people than others. And the side effects can vary depending on the type of medical marijuana used. Because of this, it's very important that anyone using medical marijuana use it with caution. People should always consult their doctor before using any form of marijuana. And they should talk to their doctor about any side effects they experience.

Whenever someone is trying to determine if a medicine is right for them, they must always consider the potential side effects. Let's look at some of the side effects of medical marijuana.

One study found that medical marijuana can reduce the symptoms of post-traumatic stress disorder by 75 percent.

Anxiety & Paranoia

Some people have severe anxiety and paranoia when using marijuana. Anxiety is a very intense and unrealistic feeling that something bad is going to happen. Paranoia is an intense and unrealistic feeling that someone is trying to hurt you. This feeling only lasts for a little while, but it is very unpleasant. People may hurt themselves or others when experiencing this side effect. Most people who have this side effect do not continue to use it. Using it could be dangerous.

Reliving Trauma

Sometimes, if something really bad happened to a person when they were little, their mind blocks it out. There have been reports of people remembering and reliving a terrible event as a side effect of using marijuana. These people also usually stop using marijuana.

Additional Common Side Effects

Other common side effects include:

- Laughing uncontrollably
- Hallucinations
- Slow reaction time
- Racing heart

- Dizziness
- Dry mouth
- Inability to drive

Some people become dependent on marijuana. This means that if they stop using it, they experience withdrawal symptoms such as:

- Irritability
- Not wanting to eat
- Inability to sleep

Addiction

Ten percent of people who use marijuana may become addicted to it. Of those who start using marijuana in their teens, 17 percent are likely to become addicted, according to the National Institute on Drug Abuse (NIDA).

Many people don't know what addiction really is. They think that just using a drug is an addiction. But addiction is a very serious brain disease. When people are addicted to something, they continue to do it even though it negatively impacts their lives. They feel like they can't stop. And when they do stop, they feel very bad until the drug is out of their system. People can reduce their risk of becoming addicted simply by understanding what addiction is and stopping use if they begin to feel addicted.

Addiction is no joke. It costs the U.S. and individuals more than $700 billion a year in treatment and healthcare costs, according to NIDA. That's a lot of money that most of us could put to much better use than having to pay for addiction treatment.

Other Health Risks

Some well-designed and large-scale studies have failed to identify any increased risk of lung cancer in people who have smoked marijuana. But the Alcohol & Drug Abuse Institute at the University of Washington reports that "no study has definitively ruled out the possibility that some individuals, especially heavier marijuana users, may incur an elevated risk of cancer. This risk appears to be smaller than for tobacco, yet is important to consider when weighing the benefits and risks of smoking marijuana." Although the association between smoking marijuana and lung cancer remains unclear, smoking a lot of medical marijuana may cause other lung problems like:

- Asthma
- Chronic Obstructive Pulmonary Disease (an umbrella term used to describe several progressive lung diseases)

- Bronchitis
- Pneumonia

Medical marijuana may also help some lung conditions, so results may vary.

Marijuana can speed up the heart rate and cause a heart attack in some people. It can also lower blood pressure to dangerous levels. People who have diabetes should only use it with caution because it can affect blood sugar levels.

Controlled Study Versus Observational Study

In this book, we'll look at several studies that show the health benefits of marijuana. To understand these, it's important to understand two science concepts: 1) controlled study and 2) observational study. Let's take a look at what these are.

Controlled Study

In a controlled study, people are divided into two or more groups. One or more groups get the substance being studied. The other group gets a placebo. A placebo is a fake version of the substance. It's sometimes called a "sugar pill." Neither group is told if they received the real thing or the placebo. This is called being blinded. The people being studied are blind to the fact that they are getting a placebo.

Scientists do experiments this way to be sure that people don't feel better just because they think they should. The human mind can play tricks on you. If you believe something enough, it can seem to be true. Scientists need to rule this out to have a highly credible study.

A controlled study can be even more credible when it's a double-blind study. This means that the test subjects don't know if they got the real substance or a placebo, and the scientists don't know which group got what either. With a double-blind study, you take out the possibility that the scientist might see what he or she wants to see. Yes, this happens to scientists, too!

Observational Study

In this type of study, also called an anecdotal study, there is no control group getting a placebo. Scientists simply observe a group of people using the substance. They then ask them questions and measure the results. This kind of study doesn't have safeguards in place to ensure that people don't just see what they want to see. They are therefore not as credible as a controlled study.

You might wonder why these studies would be done at all if they aren't reliable. They are usually done first because they are easier to do. If scientists think they are on to something, they will then do a controlled study to confirm their results. Most of the studies conducted on medical marijuana to date have been observational. That doesn't mean that they aren't good studies. It just means that scientists will need to confirm the results by doing a controlled study. Controlled studies for medical marijuana aren't easy to conduct. The reason is that if the marijuana has THC in it, people know that it's marijuana. They know because of the mind-altering effects of THC.

text-dependent questions

1. What are the two main substances in marijuana that are used for medicine?
2. What percent of people who use marijuana might become addicted to it?
3. What is a controlled study and why is it more reliable than an observational study?

research project

Get ready to learn a lot about medical marijuana in this book. You'll want to share what you learn with your friends. Get a notebook. As you read, write down some of the facts that support medical marijuana. And write down some of the reasons people are concerned about approving medical marijuana. When you finish this book, write a two-page argumentative essay in which you evaluate the facts and reach your own conclusion.

A pro-legalization marijuana parade in Toronto, Canada.

words to understand

black market: Illegally producing and selling something.

dispensaries: Stores where people can buy medical marijuana legally in some countries or in specific U.S. states.

industrial nation: A country with a highly developed economy and a high standard of living.

medical marijuana card: Similar to a driver's license. It shows that people have the legal right to use medical marijuana under the laws of their country, province, or state.

recreational use: Using marijuana for something other than treating a medical condition. This is illegal in most countries.

chapter 2

Medical Marijuana Use and Research Around the World

If you're in the United States, it's easy to see everything from a U.S. point-of-view. If you live in Canada, the United Kingdom, Jamaica, or Israel, you may view medical marijuana very differently. This is because the culture that you grow up in impacts how you see the world. People tend to see things the way the people around them do. They do not think about how other cultures may see things differently. This is called "ethnocentrism," or being ethnocentric.

As you get older, you choose to look outside of what you know. You continue to learn new things. You may even have friends on social media who live in other countries. You get to hear how they think. You get to learn what they believe. You can get more of the whole picture now. You can see many points-of-view. Ultimately, you decide for yourself what you believe. No one else can do this for you.

A nurse in a nursing home in Israel prepares medical cannabis for patients.

The Placebo Effect

The placebo effect is a term you may have heard before. It describes the fact that if people are told that a certain treatment is supposed to help them, they begin to believe that it did even if it didn't. It's all in their heads. This term originated from the fact that scientists divide study participants into two or more groups. They give placebos to one group. They give the medicine to the other. They can then compare the effects of a medicine on people who received it to the people who did not. By doing this, they can prove that their results are not just because of a placebo effect.

Exciting discoveries await those who are willing to step outside their comfort zones. It's fun to explore how other people think. You learn more about yourself and what you think you know in the process. Let's explore how other countries treat medical marijuana. And we'll look at some of the countries leading the way in medical marijuana research.

How Various Countries View & Use Medical Marijuana

Jamaica

Jamaica is an island nation in the Caribbean Sea, just off the Atlantic Ocean. It's south of Florida. The larger island of Cuba is right above it. And it's just north of Colombia in South America. Jamaica has long been believed by much of the world to welcome marijuana usage. You've probably seen the stereotypes on the internet. But actually, until 2015, marijuana usage for any reason was against the law. The tiny country spent millions on public education. It was trying to fight against its reputation. It didn't want to be seen as a marijuana haven. But that's how TV and movies continued to portray Jamaica. Today, the view has shifted. For the most part, the Jamaican government no longer sees this image as a bad thing. It has legalized the possession of small amounts of marijuana for **recreational use**. And the government is making it easier for people to get medical marijuana while in the country. Government leaders see it as a way to position the country as a wellness destination. Tourists with various conditions that marijuana is believed to treat may benefit from spending time there. If someone has a **medical marijuana card** from another country, they can easily and cheaply get a card to buy medical marijuana while in the country.

The Wellness Capital of the World

Jamaica is embracing medical marijuana. Its goal is to become the leading wellness destination in the world.

Uruguay

Uruguay is a country along the southeast side of South America. It's nestled among Brazil, Argentina, and the Atlantic Ocean. This country legalized both medical and recreational marijuana in 2013. A person can get medical marijuana at any local pharmacy. But there's a catch. Uruguay has strict rules to prevent people from using what lawmakers think is too much. Uruguayans are limited to 10 grams (.35 ounces) per week. To enforce this limit, the law requires Uruguayans to have their fingerprints scanned each time they pick up their "prescription." They must also undergo a detailed registration process. Only Uruguay citizens and legal residents can grow or buy marijuana. Such laws are in place to reduce the risk of the country becoming a tourist magnet for people who only visit to use marijuana. The country sets aside a part of the sales to help those who suffer from addiction. It also funds education programs to warn people about the risks of drug abuse.

For decades, South America has been devastated by **black market** drug growing. By legalizing but carefully regulating marijuana, Uruguay is attempting to turn something "bad" into something "good." It hopes this will reduce the damage that black market drug growing and selling has on the country and its people. The government hopes to reduce the financial burden on the country as it tries to stop drug dealers. At the same time, it's fighting against the terrible impact of illegal drug use.

PHARMACIES IN HAVE STARTED SELLING RECREATIONAL MARIJUANA

See how pharmacies in Uruguay screen people and distribute marijuana.

23

Uruguay, a small country in South America, has strict procedures for obtaining medical marijuana. Citizens must fill out lengthy forms and get fingerprinted every time they pick up their prescriptions.

Canada

In Canada, the United States' northern neighbor, medical marijuana became legal in 2001. It's grown in huge warehouses and shipped through the mail to those who qualify. **Dispensaries** are illegal in Canada. But this may change in the near future. These are the stores where medical marijuana would normally be sold. Canada has just recently completed the process of voting on a recreational marijuana bill. This bill was passed and has now become law. Under this law, recreational usage is legal as of July 1, 2018. When the law goes into effect, Canada will become the first **industrial nation** to do so. Under the law, each province will have the power to set its own minimum legal age. For example, Quebec's legal age is eighteen. Ontario's legal age is nineteen.

Israel

Israel is a small Middle Eastern country that resides among its neighbors Egypt, Jordan, Syria, and Lebanon. It borders the Mediterranean Sea. Israel was one of the first countries to legalize medical marijuana in the 1990s. But just recently the law has evolved. The government of this country made it easier for people to use medical marijuana in May 2017. Before this new law passed, medical marijuana could only be used by the patient at his or her home. Additionally, Israel "decriminalized" recreational usage in March 2017. Decriminalization is often a misunderstood word. Under this law, those who use marijuana in public can still be fined. But they will not face criminal charges. This is typically a step toward full legalization. Basically, they're saying "it's okay," but they expect their citizens to be responsible adults when using it. Teens under the legal age who are caught using marijuana without medical approval must attend a type of rehab.

In Israel, medical marijuana is quickly becoming big business. It is currently exploring a way to legally ship medical marijuana to other countries.

Learn more about marijuana research in Israel.

Denmark

Denmark is a Scandinavian country south of Norway, west of Sweden, and north of Germany. In this country, medical marijuana has been legal since 2011. But it has some very different rules. Marinol, Sativex, and Nabilone are the only approved forms of prescription medical marijuana. It's illegal for anyone to have any other kind of marijuana. This applies to even those who are approved for medical marijuana. These three drugs can only be prescribed for a very select number of conditions. The drug companies must be able to show through extensive studies that the drug benefits outweigh the side effects. A patient must receive a prescription from a neurologist to qualify for medical marijuana. A neurologist is a doctor who specializes in the treatment of the brain and the rest of the nervous system. Recreational growing, selling, and usage are all illegal. However, much like the U.S. and Canada, attitudes are changing fast.

The Netherlands

The Netherlands is located to the west of Germany and to the north of Belgium. In this country doctors can prescribe medical marijuana to patients with a set of conditions:

- Pain and spasms due to multiple sclerosis
- Nausea or loss of appetite due to AIDS
- Neurogenic pain (nerve damage)
- Tourette syndrome
- Glaucoma that cannot be otherwise treated

The War on Drugs

In the 1970s, politicians and the public became very concerned about increasing drug use in the United States. The U.S. government started a campaign called the War on Drugs. It included the famous slogan "Just say no." This campaign increased the length of prison sentences for even small-time drug offenders. It also went to war against the black-market drug growers in Central and South America. While well-intentioned, many critics today believe that it did more harm than good. Countries like Uruguay in South America are now taking a different approach as you will see.

Medical marijuana has been legal in the Netherlands since 2003. You may have heard of the city of Amsterdam before. That's in the Netherlands. Amsterdam is known for its coffee shops where people can buy very small amounts of medical marijuana to use in the shop. These coffee shops had become tourist magnets. The city did not like being known as a drug destination. In 2013, it passed laws to limit:

A coffee shop in Amsterdam, The Netherlands, where cannabis is sold.

- Who these coffee shops can sell to
- How close they can be to a school
- What hours they can operate

At the time that the Netherlands legalized medical marijuana, government officials admittedly had very little research to show its effectiveness. They only had the statements of those who said that it helped reduce their symptoms. But today, the science is beginning to catch up with the laws.

Saudi Arabia

Saudi Arabia is a Middle Eastern country. Iran is to the east. Egypt is on the west. And Iraq and Jordan are to the north. In Saudi Arabia, marijuana possession of any kind is a serious crime. Someone caught with marijuana could be put in jail for one to six months the first time they are caught. Drug dealers could get two to ten years in prison. If dealers get caught multiple times, they may go to prison for a long time or even be put to death. The United Nations Office on Drugs and Crime is an international organization that tracks drug laws around the world. It considers Saudi Arabia the third-strictest country in the world when it comes to enforcing drug laws.

What about visitors? If a visitor to Saudi Arabia tries to buy, sell, or use marijuana, he or she could face even more severe penalties.

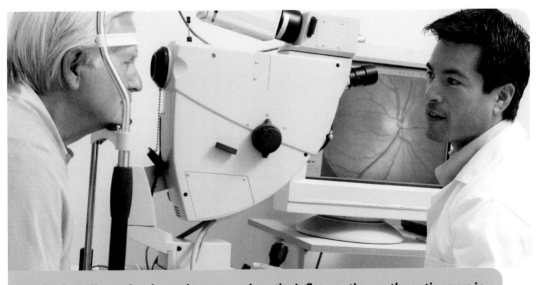

Medical marijuana has been shown to reduce the inflammation on the optic nerve in patients who have glaucoma. Above, a doctor checks a patient's eyes for glaucoma.

Approved Forms of Prescription Medical Marijuana in Denmark

Marinol, Sativex, and Nabilone are the only approved forms of medical marijuana. They are not legal for use in every country. Here is a summary of what they are used for:

Marinol is available in capsule form to help improve the appetites of those with acquired immune deficiency syndrome, as well as to help patients manage nausea and vomiting associated with cancer chemotherapy.

Sativex, an oral spray, is used to provide relief of symptoms in patients with moderate to severe spasticity due to multiple sclerosis. Spasticity is a medical condition in which certain muscles are continuously contracted.

Nabilone is available in capsule form to treat severe nausea and vomiting caused by chemotherapy treatment for cancer.

Medical Marijuana Research Around the World

Uruguay

The little South American country of Uruguay has invested time and money into removing the barriers to medical marijuana research. Before these restrictions were lifted, medical marijuana was illegal. Because of this, it was hard for scientists to study it. They couldn't actually test it on humans. Without human trials, no medicine can be proven effective through clinical trials. Since these bans were lifted, Uruguay has positioned itself as a leader in medical marijuana research. Its research will likely help other countries decide if medical marijuana has the health benefits that many claim. It will also help countries evaluate and frame their own policies related to medical usage.

The Brookings Institution is a group of researchers that offers advice on foreign policy. It believes that the studies that take place in Uruguay will either provide proof that medical marijuana is beneficial, or proof that it is not. With this proof, other countries can make better decisions about medical marijuana.

Israel

Israel is quickly positioning itself as the world leader in medical marijuana research. The Israel Ministry of Health even has a Medical Cannabis Unit dedicated to research and development. Its research goes way back. Israeli scientists were the first to discover THC in 1964. THC is the chemical in marijuana that affects the mind. More recently, their research uncovered the system in the brain that is affected by medical marijuana. They want to study this part of the brain more. They believe that they will better understand why medical marijuana has beneficial effects.

Thus far, this has been a major drawback in research around the world. People claimed to have received benefits. But it was difficult to show why they were experiencing those benefits. Without an understanding of how it worked, scientists couldn't really prove anything, Did it really relieve symptoms? Or is it simply altering one's mental state? This new research may answer those questions. Researchers in Israel believe that through this research they will be able to expand approvals for other conditions. They are researching its effects on:

- Diabetes—a disease in which the body can't effectively process sugar
- Schizophrenia—a mental disorder that can cause hallucinations and confusion
- Cancer
- Multiple sclerosis—a disease that causes a person's immune system to attack the body
- And more

Canada

In Canada, those who are trying to research medical marijuana continue to face many hurdles. There is a long application process. And it's difficult to get the various types of marijuana that need to be studied. Canada has just begun its first clinical trial on the effects of medical marijuana. Researchers are studying its effects on post-traumatic stress disorder. This is a condition that is caused by exposure to a life-threatening event such as:

- Combat exposure
- Sexual violence
- Physical assault or abuse
- Terrorist attack
- Severe accident

Researchers are also studying the impact of medical marijuana on children who have lots of seizures. And they are looking at how medical marijuana helps relieve nausea in people who feel sick during cancer treatments. Further studies are looking at how medical marijuana may help those with pain that won't go away. They also want to know if medical marijuana can help people who have osteoarthritis. This is a bone and joint disease that makes it very difficult to do normal activities.

United States

In the U.S., studying medical marijuana has historically been very difficult. Since marijuana is still considered a Schedule I drug like heroin, researchers could get in trouble if they test it on humans. Without these tests on humans, research cannot move forward. Additionally, until recently, all medical marijuana that was researched had to be grown in one place. The University of Mississippi worked with the Drug Enforcement Agency. It established a very secure facility where medical marijuana could be grown and researched. This created problems because there are many kinds of medical marijuana. The university had limited strains (or types) of marijuana. Without more expansive research, scientists could not demonstrate the beneficial effects. That's changing today as medical marijuana can now be grown and tested around the country. The challenge now is that studies take time. A study may need to last five or ten years to fully evaluate the:

- Benefits
- Side effects
- Long-term effects

Because the United States is far behind on research, it will need to rely on the research being done in other countries. The United States is closely watching Israel's findings and coordinating with researchers there in hopes of getting more solid proof regarding benefits and side effects.

text-dependent questions

1. Which country hopes to become a wellness destination for tourists?
2. Which country is considered one of the strictest in the world when it comes to any kind of marijuana usage?
3. Which country is positioning itself as the world leader in medical marijuana research?

research project

Learn more about how Uruguay is combatting the devastating effects of illegal drugs by legalizing and regulating marijuana. What does the country hope to achieve? How is this impacting the black-market drug trade in the country? Write a two-page report, answering these questions.

Studies show that cannabis is effective in reducing the symptoms of post-traumatic stress disorder (PTSD) in some patients. A woman demonstrates in support of cannabis for PTSD patients at the Global Marijuana March in Boise, Idaho.

words to understand

endocannabinoids: Chemicals that the human brain produces naturally. Similar chemicals are found in marijuana.

placebo: A fake version of a substance. Placebos are often used in medical studies; some patients get the real medicine or treatment, while others get the placebo. This is done to make sure a drug really works.

post-traumatic stress disorder: A disorder that is caused by being exposed to a life-threatening event.

schizophrenia: A disorder in which a person momentarily loses touch with reality.

chapter 3

Medical Marijuana and Mental Health

Mental health science is a relatively new field. We don't know a lot about how the mind works. In the late 1800s, Dr. Sigmund Freud introduced the idea that mental illness was the result of not getting what you want in life. He developed a process to help doctors and patients get to the root causes. In the first half of the twentieth century, doctors could do very little to help people with severe mental illnesses. They put people in institutions where the care was terrible. People usually didn't get better. In the 1960s, a medical procedure called a lobotomy became popular. People believed that if you damaged the brain a little, then mental illness could be cured. Later, people discovered that the procedure actually

More than 350 million people worldwide suffer from depression. Above, a teen talks with a counselor about her depression.

The VA Says No to Drugs

The U.S. Veteran's Administration is concerned about the number of veterans who are currently using medical marijuana to treat PTSD. It feels that the science still doesn't support it as a safe treatment.

destroyed the critical part of the brain that makes us who we are. In the 1970s, pharmaceutical companies developed drugs to relieve mental illness symptoms. Many of these drugs are still used to today. And many new ones have been developed. Will medical marijuana join them as a nationally-legal way to relieve mental health symptoms? In some countries, the answer is "yes." In others, we shall see.

In this chapter, we're going to explore how medical marijuana may help doctors treat mental health conditions. We'll look at what scientists already know. And we'll look at where they need to learn more. Let's begin.

Post-Traumatic Stress Disorder

Can medical marijuana help people with PTSD? **Post-Traumatic Stress Disorder**, or PTSD, is a mental health condition. People develop it sometimes when faced with a life-threatening situation like:

- Combat exposure
- Sexual violence
- Physical assault or abuse
- Terrorist attack
- Severe accident
- Seeing something terrible

Those with PTSD may experience what are commonly called flashbacks. During these episodes, they may "relive" the event in some way. In the case of severe PTSD, a person might actually see, hear, or feel the terrible event even though they are now safe. It can be very confusing. Because of it, they may not be able to:

- Sleep
- Eat
- Have fun

- Work
- Have friends

Medical marijuana may be the answer. Let's look at what we know.

Study Shows Marijuana May Relieve PTSD Symptoms

New Mexico is the first state in the United States to approve marijuana for treatment of PTSD. State officials based their decision on case reports like this one. A study conducted by the New Mexico Medical Cannabis Program evaluated eighty participants with PTSD over a three-year period. The participants were evaluated before they began using medical marijuana. And then they were evaluated after they had used it. The study found that patients had 75 percent fewer symptoms when they were using the medical marijuana. When they stopped using it, the symptoms returned. The study concluded with a recommendation that a controlled study is needed to confirm the results.

A Compilation Study Supports Using Medical Marijuana for PTSD

A compilation study is one that assesses the results of multiple studies about a particular topic. A medical researcher named Stephanie Yarnell, M.D., Ph.D. scoured the current studies on medical marijuana to treat PTSD. She then studied and compared the results of these studies, and she published her findings in the *Primary Care Companion for CNS Disorders.* Yarnell found that all studies that had been completed at the time were observational. She stated that there appeared to be a clear connection between medical marijuana usage and reduction in PTSD symptoms. But it could not be confirmed because the studies were not controlled. Yarnell does, however, mention that animal trials have been very promising.

Depression & Anxiety

Can medical marijuana help people with anxiety and/or depression? These are two very different conditions. But scientists often study them together because people with one often have the other as well. Depression is a mental disorder. It causes people to have overwhelming feelings of sadness. They also have lack of interest in things they once loved to do. Individuals with this disorder have trouble having fun and getting things done. The sadness makes them feel like nothing they do is ever good. They may feel like nothing good ever happens to them. Anxiety is an extreme fear of people or things in normal everyday life. Often there is no "real" reason to be afraid. But the person's body and mind are telling them to be afraid. Individuals with this condition may stay inside all the time because they are scared to go outside. They may get very nervous when they speak to people. They may constantly think that something bad is going to happen. They may worry about things they can't control. Stress that doesn't go away makes both conditions worse.

What is a Controlled Study?

In a controlled study, people are divided into two or more groups. One or more groups get the substance being studied. The other group gets a placebo. A placebo is a fake version of the substance. Neither group is told if they received the real thing or the placebo. This is called being blinded. The people being studied are blind to the fact that they are getting a placebo. Scientists do experiments this way to be sure that people don't feel better just because they think they should.

Stressed Out Rats Benefit from Marijuana

A study on rats published in *Neurotoxicity Research* found that when the brain is stressed, it produces fewer **endocannabinoids**. These chemicals help regulate thinking and emotion. Scientists believe that this may explain why people who are under a lot of stress develop depression and anxiety. The researchers gave the rats marijuana to see if it helped. As a result, the rats showed fewer symptoms. Medical marijuana is made from the cannabis plant. It has chemicals that are similar to endocannabinoids. This may also explain why using medical marijuana may reduce the signs of depression and anxiety in the rats and in humans.

Many Israeli Studies Support Benefits for Anxiety and Depression

Studies show mixed results regarding medical marijuana's effects on depression and anxiety. More human studies are needed to confirm how medical marijuana may help people with depression. We also need to have a better understanding of those who would not be helped by medical marijuana. Researchers have also been able to show that medical marijuana is a safer alternative to opioids. Opioids are a medication that is used to treat pain that won't go away. Opioids are very effective. But they're addictive, and they can cause depression and anxiety. This study found that people who used medical marijuana instead of opioids were 50 percent less likely to suffer from anxiety and depression.

Other Studies Have Not-So-Favorable Results

A study completed at King's College London showed that marijuana can actually make anxiety worse. Many test subjects experienced symptoms similar to **schizophrenia**. This is a severe mental disorder that causes patients to lose touch with reality. How could this study have such different results? The answer to this is still unknown. It's very likely that some people respond well to medical marijuana. Others do not. Another possibility is that a certain amount is safe. But too much may be harmful. These possibilities are the reason that more research is needed to understand:

1. How much to use
2. Who it works best for
3. Which types are best for which people

Insomnia

Can medical marijuana help people with insomnia? This condition causes a person to not be able to go to sleep or stay asleep most nights. It may be connected to:

- PTSD
- Depression
- Anxiety
- Other disorders

A lot has changed recently in the world of medical marijuana. In 2012, a sleep researcher and psychologist, John Cline Ph.D., published an article in *Psychology Today*. He proclaimed that

Each year, researchers find more uses for medical marijuana.

How Common Is Depression?

More than 350 million people worldwide suffer from depression, according to the World Health Organization. Sixteen million people have severe depression that impacts their ability to function most days. Could medical marijuana be the answer? Maybe. Maybe not.

there was no evidence to show that medical marijuana could help insomnia. Fast forward to 2017, Dr. Cline began to rethink his position and stated that it was time to take a closer look.

Marijuana May Cause Insomnia

A Boston University School of Public Health study evaluated ninety-eight people. Researchers divided them into three groups:

- Daily users (49)
- Occasional users (29)
- Non-users (20)

This study found that heavy marijuana use may be disruptive to sleep. Daily users were more likely to have sleep problems. In fact, twice as many daily users had sleep problems as non-users. It's unclear from this study if the marijuana caused the sleep problems. Perhaps the subjects were using it because they had sleep problems already.

But Others May Benefit

In a study published in the *Hawai'i Journal of Medicine & Public Health,* researchers found something very different. They were able to show that people who use marijuana have 45 percent fewer symptoms when using marijuana. Why do you think that this study may differ? More research is needed for us to understand why.

Addiction/Opioid Crisis

Can medical marijuana help people who are addicted to "more harmful" drugs like unpre-scribed opioids? Opioids are drugs that affect the nervous system to relieve pain. Some opioids are legal in the United States. But you must have a prescription. You may have heard of some of them:

- Morphine
- Codeine
- Vicodin
- Oxycodone

When prescribed by a doctor and used responsibly, these medicines can help people. They reduce serious pain that doesn't go away. But there's also a dark side. These drugs are very addictive. A doctor may prescribe the drugs, but people may become addicted while using them. When their prescriptions run out, they may continue to buy the drugs on the black market (a place where goods and services are illegally produced and sold). Additionally, people who have never been prescribed these drugs may be offered them by a so-called

Medical marijuana can reduce insomnia in some patients.

Sleepless Nights

Treating sleep disorders like insomnia is big business in the United States. Analysts forecast that it will become a $3 billion industry by 2025. Researchers estimate that as much as 15 percent of the U.S. population has some form of insomnia. They can't fall sleep or stay asleep. In our fast-paced world where so many people are stressed out, people are looking for answers. Could medical marijuana solve their problems?

A mural in Vancouver, Canada, commemorates the lives of those who died from fentanyl and opioid overdoses.

friend. No real friend would ever encourage a friend to use these drugs. They are very dangerous.

The Opioid Crisis

Drug overdose is the leading cause of accidental death in the United States. In 2015, there were 52,404 lethal drug overdoses, according to the Centers for Disease Control. Opioid addiction caused a majority of these deaths; there were 20,101 overdose deaths related to prescription pain relievers, and 12,990 overdose deaths related to heroin. Opioid addiction devastates families, children, and communities. Opioid abuse is also a problem in other countries such as Canada, Norway, Greece, Denmark, Finland, Estonia, and Australia. Most people who are addicted to opioids find themselves unable to quit without a lot of help from family and professionals.

Learn more about the opioid crisis in the United States.

Medical Marijuana May Be an Answer

Like the rest of the U.S., opioid addiction and deaths were on the rise in Colorado. But something happened in 2014 that seems to have changed this course—Colorado legalized recreational marijuana. When it did, the state saw a 6 percent annual decrease in opioid deaths. And the death rate continues to decline. A study published in the *American Journal of Public Health* showed just that. Researchers believe that this shows that if people are given a choice, they will choose marijuana instead of opioids. We should note that marijuana still has side effects, as we'll discuss. But the side effects are much less extreme. This provides us with a real-world example of how medical marijuana could help those suffering from addiction.

Overall Relaxation

Can medical marijuana help people relax? According to the *Chicago Tribune,* 40 percent of marijuana users say that they use it to relax. But is there science to support this? Very few studies have been done at this time to determine if marijuana can help people relax. But let's look at a controlled study.

Double-Blind Controlled Study Says "Sometimes"

A controlled study conducted at the University of Illinois at Chicago looked at forty-two participants. Researchers divided the people into three groups. One group was given a high dose. The second group received a low dose. The third group was given a **placebo**. Researchers put the participants into a high-stress situation. It involved:

- Giving a speech
- Having to answer basic math questions quickly in front of people
- Being recorded
- Watching the video live as it happens

Who wouldn't be stressed in this situation?

The scientists gauged how stressed the people were. The study found that the people taking the low dose felt less stressed than the people taking the placebo. But the people taking the high dose felt more stressed than either group. What do you think this study concluded? It concluded that very low doses may allow people to relax. But larger doses have the opposite effect. This study was controlled. Remember, that's a good thing. But it does have some critics who point out that:

- They didn't use the whole plant. THC alone may not be what helps people relax.
- Participants ate the THC. Some believe that it's different if taken in by the lungs.
- Some types of marijuana may increase stress. Others may decrease it.

Overdose Dangers for Those with Mental Disorders

It's like this with so many things in life. Something may help a person in small doses. But it may hurt them if they use too much. This has been shown to be true with medical marijuana. We've already looked at one example of this in the last section. Let's look at some more.

Marijuana Overdose

Marijuana overdose is different from overdose from opioids or cocaine. The part of the brain that responds to marijuana doesn't control life functions like breathing. As far as science knows at this time, people don't die from marijuana overdose directly. But that doesn't mean that it's not dangerous in high doses. You can still overdose. An overdosing person may experience:

- Panic attacks
- Uncontrolled shaking
- Unresponsiveness (passed out or zombie-like)
- Rapid heartbeat
- High blood pressure

Even if a person doesn't overdose, a person might take a very high dose that impacts their ability to:

- Follow pedestrian rules
- Follow driving rules
- Stay out of dangerous situations
- Obey laws

Any of these could get the person seriously hurt or killed. Someone might also use so much that they make other bad decisions:

- Skipping school
- Not going to work
- Neglecting health
- Replacing interaction with people with the use of marijuana
- Hurting people

These may not immediately kill the person, but they could very slowly destroy his or her life.

Mental Conditions that Call for Restricted Marijuana Use

People with certain conditions may have bad effects when using even a little marijuana. They should be cautious or be closely monitored by a doctor. These conditions include:

- Depression
- Anxiety
- PTSD

Learn more about how marijuana can impact those with bipolar disorder.

Also, people with the following should be careful:

- Bipolar disorder
- Schizophrenia
- Severe trauma (e.g., physical abuse, mental abuse)

The fact remains that everyone is different. One person may be helped. Another may not be helped. We need more studies to determine who should use medical marijuana, and who should not.

text-dependent questions

1. Why do scientists believe that medical marijuana may have helped the "stressed out rats"?
2. In 2014, what happened in Colorado at the same time that opioid death rates dropped in that state?
3. What are three possible effects of using too much marijuana?

research project

Learn more about the dangers of using too much medical marijuana. Get a poster board and images from the internet. Create a visual aid that shows some of the harmful effects of using too much marijuana.

Medical marijuana is being used to treat the side effects of many diseases of the immune system.

words to understand

anecdotal evidence: Evidence that's based on one or more person's personal experiences rather than a study.

immune system: The system in your body that protects you against infections.

malnutrition: Not getting enough nutrition to stay healthy; a common side effect of many diseases.

side effects: Bad (adverse) or good (therapeutic) things that can happen to a person after he or she takes a medication or undergoes a medical treatment.

chapter 4

Medical Marijuana and Physical Health

The human body is a complex network of systems. When one system doesn't work right, it can make the rest of the body sick. There are many medications to help people who are sick. But these medications often have severe **side effects**. Whenever someone is using any kind of medication, they must always ask themselves an important question. Is taking this medication worth these side effects? Often the answer is "no." As we discussed in the last chapter, medical marijuana also has side effects. But for many people, the side effects are more tolerable than those of their prescribed medications. For this reason, people turn to medical

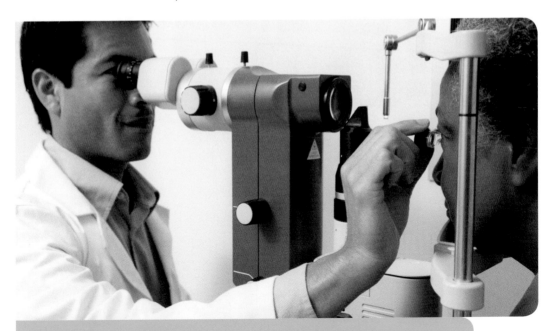

Medical marijuana is being used to reduce the severe pressure in the eyes of those with glaucoma. Above, a doctor checks a patient for glaucoma.

marijuana to relieve their symptoms without the bad side effects. Let's explore some of the diseases for which medical marijuana may be able to relieve symptoms. And we'll look at some of the studies that support using medical marijuana for these and similar conditions.

Immune System Diseases

Your **immune system** protects your body from invaders such as viruses and bacteria. But sometimes things go wrong. It may overrespond, causing inflammation disorders such as asthma or arthritis. We'll talk about inflammation separately a little later. Sometimes the immune system stops working very well. That's what happens with HIV/AIDS. And sometimes the immune system thinks that a person's own cells are the invaders. It attacks those cells and destroys them. This can cause terrible damage to the body. Let's look at three immune system diseases that marijuana may help, in addition to others.

Medical marijuana is being used to help treat people with severe migraines, such as this woman.

Suicide Rates High for Those with MS

Multiple sclerosis (MS) is a disease that causes a lot of pain and an inability to control the body. Once diagnosed, the average person only lives about twenty-five more years. These years are often spent in extreme pain. For some, the pain is too much. The suicide rate among people with MS is 7.5 times higher than it is for the general public, according to the National Multiple Sclerosis Society.

Multiple Sclerosis

In multiple sclerosis (MS), the immune system attacks the nerves. Nerves transfer signals to the brain about the world around us. But when these nerves are damaged, the signals become distorted. Those with the condition get terrible muscle spasms, among other symptoms.

In a controlled study published in the *Canadian Medical Association Journal,* researchers observed thirty people with MS who hadn't responded well to other medications. Half the group was given a placebo. The other half used marijuana. They found that participants in the marijuana group had one-third fewer muscle spasms than those in the placebo group. This promising study demonstrates that patients with this disease may be able to get some relief from marijuana. A CB2 receptor is a part of your immune system that helps regulate the immune system response. Studies show that the substances in marijuana bind to the CB2 receptors. By doing this, they can help reduce the effects of an overactive immune system. This is likely what reduces the symptoms.

HIV/AIDS

HIV is a virus that attacks a person's immune system. If left uncontrolled, it will become AIDS. When it does, it will destroy this system. Without the immune system to protect a person, he or she will get very sick. People with this disease have common symptoms like:

- Pain
- Nausea
- Not wanting to eat

When Even Eating Causes Pain

Approximately 1.6 million people in the United States have inflammatory bowel disorder, according to the Crohn's & Colitis Foundation. Most are diagnosed before age thirty-five. For these individuals, even the act of eating food can be painful. Their digestive systems can't properly break down food and absorb nutrients.

These symptoms cause people who have AIDS to lose weight very fast until their bodies can't go on. Medical marijuana has been shown to help people with HIV/AIDS in several ways. It relieves nausea in patients with HIV/AIDs. It increases appetite so that they want to eat again. It can help control pain. It may also help with depression and insomnia in some people.

Lupus

Lupus is another disease in which the immune system thinks that healthy cells are invaders. It produces too many antibodies, which are like natural "antibiotics" that fight infection. But when there are too many of them, they overwhelm the body. Pain, inflammation, and damage result.

There are prescription drugs for lupus. But these drugs make the immune system very weak. People who use these medications get lots of infections. They're helpless against typically harmless viruses like colds.

Substances found in marijuana can help reduce this inflammation and damage by blocking some of the antibodies from being released.

Glaucoma

Glaucoma is a disease in the optic nerve of one's eye. This nerve is responsible for carrying visual signals from the eye to the brain. Those with glaucoma experience incredible pressure in the eye called interocular pressure. Over time this pressure can cause loss of vision. To treat glaucoma, this pressure must be reduced.

Can Medical Marijuana Benefit Those with Glaucoma?

Medical marijuana has been shown to reduce the inflammation on the optic nerve in patients who have glaucoma. But there's a catch. Patients only experience a pressure reduction for three to four hours. After that, the pressure goes back up. Any pressure causes eye damage. Patients need to use the medical marijuana every three to four hours. This requires taking medical marijuana six to eight times a day. That's considered a lot. Who wants to have to remember to take medicine eight times a day? Because of this, it may not be a good option for some patients. Researchers are investigating high-potency THC eye drops. They hope that this will provide a better option for patients.

Inflammation

Inflammation results from an overactive immune system. Diseases that end in "-itis" are inflammatory diseases like:

- Colitis: inflammation of the colon (large intestine)
- Arthritis: joint inflammation
- Bronchitis: inflammation of the bronchial tubes (part of your respiratory system)
- Sinusitis: sinus inflammation
- Hepatitis: liver inflammation.

Diabetes Can Make People Go Blind

People with Type II diabetes have trouble processing sugar in their bodies. Sudden sugar spikes and drops can cause long-term harm to their bodies. Those who don't exercise and are overweight are more likely to develop this condition. Approximately twenty-nine million people in the U.S. suffer from it, according to the Centers for Disease Control and Prevention. Worldwide, about 422 million people had diabetes in 2014, according to the World Health Organization. As technology makes our lives easier, we're moving less. Many countries around the world are battling this terrible disease. Because of this disease, people may develop other dangerous conditions, like glaucoma. Glaucoma causes there to be high pressure behind a person's eyes. If they don't keep this pressure down, they can go blind.

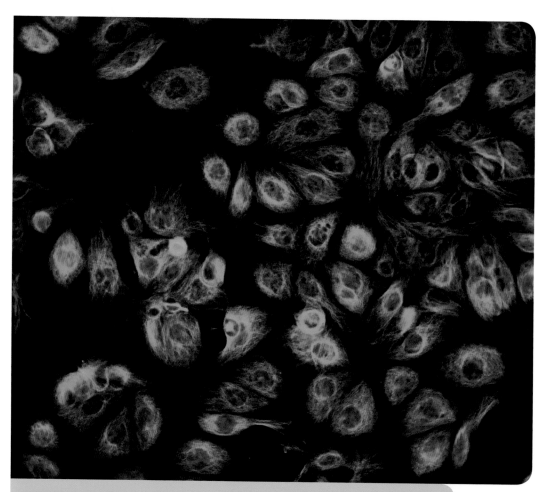

Medical marijuana can help reduce nausea, weight loss, and other symptoms experienced by people who have cancer. Above, cancer cells imaged with a fluorescence microscope.

Some other common inflammatory diseases that don't include "-itis" are:

- Celiac disease: inflammation that impacts the small intestine
- Fibromyalgia: nerve inflammation
- Inflammatory bowel disease: inflammation of the intestines
- Asthma: inflammation that causes breathing problems.

Can Medical Marijuana Benefit Those with Inflammation?

Studies have long shown that medical marijuana can reduce inflammation for many inflammatory diseases. A study published in *Rheumatology* looked at fifty-eight patients with rheumatoid arthritis. They were split into two groups. The marijuana group experienced significant pain reduction. The placebo group did not.

Crohn's Disease

Crohn's disease is a very severe inflammatory disease in the lower small intestine and top of the large intestine. It may result in:

- Severe diarrhea
- Bleeding
- Urgent need to use the washroom
- Cramps

A study performed in Israel (and detailed in the *Israel Medical Association Journal*) looked at thirty people with Crohn's. Researchers interviewed patients regarding their experiences over the ten years before they started the study. They asked about and documented:

- Number of surgeries
- Symptoms
- Hospitalizations
- Severity of disease based upon an index
- Medication doses

They then had the thirty patients use medical marijuana for three years. Twenty-one of the thirty improved while using the marijuana. The patients were able to drastically reduce how much medication they were taking. Before the patients began treatment, fifteen of them had had to have surgeries, which is common for Crohn's. During treatment, only three had to have surgery.

To strengthen the findings of the study, two years later they divided the twenty-one patients into two groups. The eleven-person group received real marijuana. They gave the other group a placebo. Five of the eleven people using the real marijuana got rid of all their symptoms. Only one of the ten using the placebo found relief during the same time. This suggests that the marijuana played a significant role in eliminating the Crohn's symptoms. But more studies are needed to confirm this.

How Do Drugs Get Approved by the FDA?

For a drug to be approved by the Food & Drug Administration (FDA), scientists must be able to prove that it's both safe and effective for specific conditions. If the drug is not deemed to be effective for a certain condition, then doctors can't prescribe it for that diagnosis. And someone selling it cannot legally claim that it prevents or treats that condition.

Muscle Spasms

Muscle spasms have many different causes. A muscle could be dehydrated (not have enough water content to work properly). It could be overworked. Or it could be tired. Some people have eye or face twitches when they're stressed out. That's a muscle spasm. But some muscle spasms are constant and very painful. A person's muscles suddenly contract and jerk. Sometimes they can't walk, eat, or even hold a pen in their hand. These may be caused by a disease passed down through the family. Or someone may have been in a terrible accident that caused a brain or spinal cord injury.

General Muscle Spasms

Researchers have extensively studied the effects of medical marijuana on muscle spasms in animals. Small doses of medical marijuana have demonstrated an ability to reduce muscle spasms. There is also significant **anecdotal evidence** that marijuana can reduce muscle spasms in humans. Anecdotal means that the evidence is self-reported rather than the result of a study.

Muscle spasms are associated with severe diseases you may have heard of like Leeuwenhoek's Disease or multiple sclerosis (MS). We already discussed MS, so let's look at how medical marijuana may benefit those with Leeuwenhoek's Disease.

Leeuwenhoek's Disease

This disease causes the lungs to spasm and collapse uncontrollably. People with this disease feel like they're hyperventilating. It's very painful because the spasms won't stop. Think about the worst case of hiccups you've ever had and multiply it by one hundred. Now, imagine it happening every day, about twelve times a day. Get the picture? This is a rare disease so it's very hard to study enough people with it. But studies of single individuals with the disease have shown that marijuana can reduce attacks and stop an attack as it happens.

Pain

Pain doesn't need much explanation. Everyone has felt it. But some pain doesn't go away even after the body has healed. When pain doesn't go away people need medicine to relieve the pain so that they can study, work, sleep, and enjoy life. Studies have shown that medical marijuana can help reduce pain for people who have pain that won't go away. We have significant anecdotal evidence that marijuana relieves pain. But what do the controlled studies say? Let's take a look. One study involved twenty-one people. They rotated these people through four different treatment options. These included:

- Moderately high doses of THC
- Mid-level dose of THC
- Low dose of THC
- Placebo

The patients were not told which one they were using. The high dose group had around an 8 percent reduction in pain. The results of the study were discussed in *Medical Cannabis: Evidence on Efficacy,* from the District of Columbia Department of Health. Other studies support modest pain relief from medical marijuana. But for people who are always in pain, any relief is often a reason to seek treatment.

Watch a video that shows how cannabis oil helped a little girl who was having seven-hundred seizures a day.

Seizures

What do you think of when you hear the word "electricity"? You might think of lights and devices that need it to work. You might think about that time when you stuck something into an electrical socket and got shocked. Humans also have electrical waves moving through their bodies. These electrical impulses normally transfer messages between the brain and rest of the body. People with seizures experience a sudden and prolonged burst of electricity in their brains. This surge causes thousands of messages to be sent out at once. It overloads the human body. As a result, a person with seizures shakes uncontrollably until the seizure stops. Some seizures only affect one part of the body. Others cause complete loss of control of the body. Injuries are very common. People with seizures often have trouble going to school, working, or participating in activities you may take for granted. They have very little warning before an episode. Some people have dozens of these a week. The main disease that causes seizures is called epilepsy.

Learn more about Alexis Bortell's struggle to gain access to a life-changing medicine to fight her seizures.

Can Medical Marijuana Reduce Epilepsy Symptoms?

Epilepsy is one of the conditions in which we've seen the most proof that medical marijuana is beneficial. People with epilepsy who once had many seizures a day have few or none while using medical marijuana. Such is the case with twelve-year-old Alexis Bortell. Alexis once had several seizures every week, according to a report in *Rolling Stone*. She now takes a few drops of liquid THC every time she feels a seizure about to start. With this treatment, she hasn't had a single seizure in two years. Alexis can now do all the things that teenagers should be able to do. She can safely go to school and play with friends. She can even get her driver's license in a few years. Alexis has become the voice for many people like her. She was invited to speak to the congress of the United States. She works as an activist to change the federal laws regarding medical marijuana. Because of cases like hers, more people in the United States can now get medical marijuana for epilepsy and other diseases.

Can Medical Marijuana Reduce Dravet's Symptoms?

Dravet's is a rare type of epilepsy caused by a mutation in one of a person's genes. Genes are passed down to a baby from his or her mother and father when a baby is growing in a mother's belly. They tell your eyes what color they're supposed to be. They tell your skin what shade it will be. And sometimes they also have a mutation that makes someone have a disease. Children with Dravet's first start getting seizures around age one. If they aren't treated, these seizures damage the brain. But there are no approved treatments for Dravet's.

Children with Dravet's and other types of epilepsy often receive CBD oil. CBD is a part of the medical marijuana plant that doesn't have the mental effects. A study published in the *New England Journal of Medicine* showed that CBD oil can cut the number of seizures in a child with Dravet's in half. Five percent of those studied stopped having seizures completely. The placebo group in this study had no significant reduction. This study is yet another example that demonstrates the medicinal value of medical marijuana.

Cancer

Many of us know someone who has had cancer in the past, or has cancer now. But do you know what cancer is? Your body is made up of trillions of cells. You have lung cells and heart cells. You have cells that make taste buds. You have cells that form your bones. Each cell is a living thing. That's why you need to feed your cells with healthy food. These cells have a lifespan. Some cells live a few days. Others live for months. When cells die, they must be replaced by new cells. Healthy cells have the ability to divide themselves into two to make a new cell. Cancer is a cell. When cancer cells are in the body, they divide very fast. These cancer cells start to outnumber the good cells.

To get rid of the cancer, people usually have to have chemotherapy or radiation treatment. These treatments attempt to kill these cancer cells. The problem is that it's hard to kill these cancer cells without also damaging other cells in the body. That's why people get so sick. Most cancer symptoms aren't from the cancer itself, they're from the treatments. People receiving these treatments suffer from similar symptoms such as:

- Nausea/vomiting
- Loss of appetite
- Weight loss
- **Malnutrition**

Medical marijuana can reduce these symptoms. The American Cancer Society supports the fact that some compounds in marijuana can ease these symptoms. Studies have shown that it can reduce nausea and vomiting in those with cancer. It also has a well-known ability to increase appetite. This helps cancer patients get more of the nutrients they need to stay healthier during treatments.

Marijuana has been shown to reduce symptoms for many other diseases that cause similar symptoms to the ones we've discussed in this chapter. It's important to realize that there are many different types, or strains, of marijuana. Different types have different amounts of the various symptom-reducing substances like CBD and THC. Some people may benefit more from one that has more of a certain substance than another. People may also respond differently based on how they consume it. Some people eat marijuana or take it in pill form. Others might inhale it as smoke or mixed in water vapor. These factors could explain why some people find relief through medical marijuana and others don't. As scientists continue to study these substances, we'll better understand how to give each patient what they need to feel better.

1. What's the name of the receptor in your brain that medical marijuana blocks to reduce the effects of an overactive immune system?
2. All diseases that end in the suffix "-itis" have what in common?
3. Name five symptoms that medical marijuana may reduce in patients with the diseases we discussed in this chapter.

research project

Learn more about how teens like Alexis Bortell and their families are impacting marijuana policy in the United States by telling their stories. Find three similar cases. Write a two-page paper that showcases how their stories are impacting medical marijuana laws in the United States.

Taxes from the sales of medical marijuana are being used to fund road construction projects.

words to understand

human trials: Studies that are done on human beings. Animal studies can only tell us so much. We need human trials to understand how substances impact humans.

lawmakers: A general term for people who help decide what the laws will be in a city, state, province, country, etc.

personal responsibility: Making personal choices regarding your own health, life, and future.

tax revenues: The amount of money collected by taxing something like income or sales of certain items.

chapter 5

The Future of Medical Marijuana

What's the future of medical marijuana? Will more countries approve it? What might their laws look like? Let's consider what we already know and have discussed in this book as we look at what may happen in the next five to ten years.

Lawmakers Take a Closer Look

In 2016, **lawmakers** in Nashville, Tennessee, in the United States, met to discuss the future of medical marijuana in their state. States all over the country are holding similar meetings to weigh the issue. They need to explore, among other things:

- Research
- Policies
- Jobs
- Taxes
- Federal law
- Public safety

Like those who've gone before them, they're looking closely at the states and countries that have already approved medical marijuana. They're figuring out what a medical marijuana registry would look like in their state. Let's take a look at what they talked about.

Hearing Experts & Getting Answers

During these sessions, they hear from doctors and other industry experts. They get to ask questions and share their concerns. They want to know:

- Does science really support the benefits that people claim?
- Do the benefits outweigh the side effects?
- What policies need to be in place to prevent abuse?

Job Growth Potential Considered

Many in the meeting see more than an opportunity to help people who are sick. They see the medical marijuana's potential to bring jobs to the state. Medical marijuana sales totaled nearly $7 billion in the United States, according to the cannabis industry research firm Arcview Market Research. The industry may earn $20.2 billion by 2021. Legalizing medical use would potentially add more jobs for people in the state in:

- Dispensaries
- Farming
- Manufacturing
- Transportation
- Marketing/advertising
- Finance
- Security
- Legal
- Regulation

That's good for the state economy and the people of Tennessee.

Find out how the marijuana industry is transforming the economy of the desert town of California City, California.

Tax Revenues Considered

When something is being sold on the black market, it can't be taxed. Many argue that states who do not legalize marijuana are losing money that they could gain by legalizing and taxing marijuana. **Tax revenues** help pay for things we need like:

A window of a coffee shop in Amsterdam displays a huge variety of cannabis products.

That's a Lot of Marijuana

There are nearly 800 types of marijuana plants, according to the *Los Angeles Times*. As studies continue, we'll better understand which plants are best for treating certain conditions, have fewer side effects, etc.

- Roads
- Schools
- Healthcare
- Law enforcement
- Programs that help the poor
- And a lot more

People who want to see marijuana legalized in states like Tennessee point out that once it's legal, it will bring much-needed money into the state. Colorado, for example, has raised more than $500 million in taxes since legalizing recreational marijuana in 2014.

Federal Law Concerns

Doctors can't prescribe medical marijuana in the United States. It's still illegal under federal law. It hasn't been approved by the Food & Drug Administration (FDA). That's the agency that approves medications for treatments of certain conditions. It has very strict guidelines for approval. And the studies done so far have yet to meet its standards.

Some people in the meeting feel that Tennessee should wait until it's legal across the United States. But others argue that with over half of the states in the U.S. already having a comprehensive medical marijuana law, there's no reason to wait. It's just a matter of time. Besides, they argue, it's their right as a state.

In the United States, state law overrules federal law for many things. It's in the U.S. Constitution—check it out. Therefore, medical marijuana can be legal in a state like Colorado, Washington, or New Mexico, but illegal outside of that state.

Public Safety Concerns

Some argue that legalizing medical marijuana will put a strain on law enforcement. They look at the opioid addiction struggles facing the nation. They see medical marijuana as possibly causing the same kinds of problems. Others look to countries like Uruguay. Remember, it made marijuana legal to combat black market drug crimes. Perhaps legalizing it will reduce drug crime. Still others point out Colorado, where opioid deaths continue to fall after it legalized marijuana.

Many things that are legal—such as alcohol—can be harmful, or deadly, if not used responsibly.

The Outcome

These things and more will be considered as this state evaluates whether it will become one of the next states to approve medical marijuana. Meetings like this one have been going on around the United States and around the world. They're shaping the laws of today and paving the way for the future of medical marijuana.

Better Research

As nations reduce the barriers in place that have long reduced the ability of scientists to properly study medical marijuana, we'll see more definitive studies. Let's look at what those studies may find.

More Human Trials

For some time, performing a study using humans has been difficult. Researchers had trouble getting access to marijuana. They couldn't legally give people marijuana. They were very limited regarding the types of marijuana they could test. Because **human trials** were so restricted, it was difficult to conduct trials that would prove what people were claiming.

That's changing. Today and into the near future it will be easier to perform human trials. Scientists who have gotten certain results with rats will now be able to see if the same is true for humans. The human studies will give us a clearer picture of how medical marijuana works and who it can help. It will confirm the therapeutic value of marijuana especially to:

- Control nausea/vomiting
- Stimulate appetite
- Reduce seizures
- Suppress spasms
- Eliminate inflammation

From these studies, we'll learn to appreciate how fast marijuana works to relieve symptoms. Some medications can take hours, days, or weeks to provide similar relief.

Studying Various Types of Marijuana & What It's Made of

The different types of marijuana have different amounts of the medicinal substances. Some types of marijuana, or marijuana substances, may be better for some people or some diseases. Through these human trials, we'll better understand which patients will benefit from which types of marijuana. This will include studying cannabis oils that don't have THC in them. You'll recall that THC is the substance that has the mental side effects. It will also

Bad Science

Around 70 percent of researchers say they've tried to reproduce the results from the studies of other scientists, but found something completely different. This statistic points out why so many studies are needed to confirm the benefits or side effects of any medicinal drug. Scientists must look at the whole picture. They must look at how each study was done and whether it can be repeated. Many studies that looked promising get thrown out or have to be redone. But as a result, we have a truer picture of how a therapeutic drug like medical marijuana can really help people.

include developing a better understanding of THC and its effects. Through new research, people will continue to separate the fact from the fiction about marijuana. Society will recognize that if THC is needed to improve the quality of life of someone suffering from a terrible disease, then it's worth the side effects.

More Controlled Studies

With fewer restrictions, we'll continue to see more controlled studies. Many of these studies have already begun. They will be completed over the next several years. Do you remember what controlled studies are? These are the studies that have one or more groups receiving marijuana. They then have a third group who thinks that they are, but they're really getting a placebo. These studies help us confirm definitively if medical marijuana is really benefiting people. Government entities like the FDA in the United States will review these studies to determine whether doctors can begin prescribing marijuana as a medication.

Better Understanding of How Marijuana Relieves Symptoms

Ongoing studies in Israel, Canada, Uruguay, and elsewhere will help us better understand how and why medical marijuana works. This is important because critics state that all it does is "get people high." They think that being high is the only reason that people get relief. Over the next several years, science will need to show that the improvements in symptoms are not just the result of the mental effects of the drug. Based on the studies conducted, scientists believe that being high has very little to do with the relief that people experience. More controlled studies will soon prove that.

A Clearer Understanding of the Side Effects

We'll also have a clearer understanding of the side effects such as slow response time and not thinking clearly right after using marijuana. With this new knowledge, we'll be able to develop treatment plans that reduce the side effects. But they still allow people to get the benefits. Out of this will likely come healthier ways to get the benefits. Currently, smoking medical marijuana is common. There are some studies that show that smoking marijuana is much less harmful than smoking cigarettes. But it's still smoking. Science will continue to develop other ways to get the benefits like:

- Oils
- Eye drops
- Skin creams
- Pills
- Injections

Many of these are already in the works or available in some areas.

Bringing Bad Science to Light

Over the past several years, many studies have claimed to find many different things. This has led to claims that medical marijuana can treat so many different diseases. As more studies are completed, we'll undoubtedly find out that some of the studies were flawed. This happens all the time in science. Sometimes a study can't be duplicated. Or another, more thorough study, proves that the first study was wrong. When this happens, scientists must look at all the studies together. They can then get a better picture. We may find out that medical marijuana doesn't have benefits for some of the conditions we've talked about. But at the same time, we may discover new conditions that medical marijuana can help. It's all part of the scientific process. You'll have the opportunity to see how this develops and what we find out.

Legalization Across the World

As studies continue to prove the benefits of medical marijuana and how best to regulate it, we'll see more countries legalizing it. Even some countries where the use of marijuana is a serious crime, like Saudi Arabia, may decide it's okay for medical use. These countries may take different approaches. But they'll continue to look to those before them to decide what their laws should be. As countries begin to figure out what laws work best, we may see places that have already approved it going back and updating their laws. As an example of what may happen around the world, let's look at three options that might occur in the U.S. in the next five to ten years.

Marijuana Becomes Schedule II

Marijuana is currently a Schedule I drug in the United States. This means that it's classified as highly addictive and illegal. These drugs are said to have no medical use. We may see marijuana be changed to a Schedule II drug at the federal level. Schedule II drugs are prescription drugs that can be very addictive. They have strong physical and psychological effects. But they're considered okay if a doctor monitors the patient to avoid abuse. Other schedule II drugs include Vicodin, Percocet, Oxycodone, and Ritalin. If marijuana becomes a Schedule II drug, people would have to have a prescription from their doctor to purchase it. This would continue to restrict recreational marijuana use to the states where it's legal. But it would eliminate the barriers for the sick people who marijuana could help.

Marijuana Can Be Bought Over the Counter with Registration

One other route that the U.S. could go is making some or all marijuana legal to purchase without a prescription. But in this option, it wouldn't be like buying Tylenol. The government would require that people sign up. They may also require fingerprinting and quantity limits. This would be similar to Uruguay's laws.

The U.S. has current laws regarding the purchase of Sudafed (Pseudoephedrine), a nasal decongestant. Pseudoephedrine is also used by criminals to make crystal meth, a harmful street drug. To battle the making and selling of meth, federal law limits how much Sudafed a person can buy. Marijuana law could reflect Sudafed law. Marijuana law could become like this.

Marijuana Becomes Fully Legal

Finally, marijuana could become fully legal without a prescription. If people feel sick to their stomachs, they might walk into a dispensary and buy it like they were buying Tylenol. If this were to occur, it's very likely that there would be an age limit like Canada's. **Personal responsibility** would be fully on the person buying and using it. They would need to use it responsibly to avoid the negative side effects of using too much. That leads us to our next point.

Education

Marijuana may be natural, but it's not harmless. It's very important that we realize that as we continue to see more places making it legal. Many things that are legal can be harmful, or deadly, if not used responsibly, like:

- Guns
- Knives

- Alcohol
- Vehicles
- Sleeping pills

Just like drinking alcohol or taking too much Ibuprofen, too much marijuana can be harmful. And some people may find that they can't use it because of how it affects them. They need to realize this and avoid it for their own personal health. It will be important that people around the world get informed about the dangers of using too much. Like all things in life, people will still have to be responsible to avoid getting hurt. We'll likely see more public education about how to make smart choices when using marijuana.

text-dependent questions

1. What are three ways that medical marijuana may benefit places that legalize it, in addition to helping sick people?
2. What are two specific things we hope to better understand about medical marijuana through human trials?
3. How does personal responsibility factor into one's choice about how much marijuana to use or whether to use it at all?

research project

How do you see the future of marijuana in your country, state, or city? With a partner, design a presentation that explores the future of medical marijuana. Be creative. Dress up and role-play if you'd like. Include visual aids and share your thoughts and ideas with your class.

series glossary of key terms

adult-use cannabis: The recreational use of cannabis by those over the age of twenty-one.

cannabidiol (CBD): A chemical compound found in the cannabis plant that is non-psycho-active. It is known for its medical and pain relief properties.

cannabinoid: Any of various chemical compounds (such as THC) from the cannabis or marijuana plant that produces a euphoric feeling, or "high."

cannabis clubs: Marijuana growing and consumption cooperatives (a group that is owned and run by its members) that exist in countries such as Uruguay and Spain to provide cannabis users with marijuana products and a place to use those products.

cannabis strains: Varieties of cannabis plants that are developed to have different properties and potencies.

clinical trials: Experiments with unproven medications that may or may not help a patient get better.

dabbing: A somewhat controversial method of cannabis flash-vaporization. It has very strong effects on the user.

decriminalization: The legal term for getting rid of or reducing criminal charges for having or using cannabis.

delta-9-tetrahydrocannabinol (THC): A natural chemical compound found in the flowers of the marijuana plant. It produces a feeling of euphoria and a psychoactive reaction, or "high," when marijuana is eaten or smoked.

dopamine: A naturally occurring chemical in the human body that increases pleasurable feelings in the mind and body.

drug trafficking: A global illegal trade involving the growth, manufacture, distribution, and sale of substances, such as cannabis, that are subject to drug prohibition laws.

edible: A food made or infused (cooked or otherwise prepared) with cannabis extracts (portions of the plant, including seeds or flowers).

endocannabinoid system: A group of cannabinoid receptors found in the brain and central and peripheral nervous systems of mammals that help control appetite, pain, mood, and memory.

euphoria: A feeling of intense well-being and happiness.

extracts: Portions of the marijuana plant, including seeds or flowers.

hash: A solid or resinous extract of cannabis.

hemp: A cannabis plant grown for its fiber and used to make rope, textiles, paper, and other products.

ingest: To take food, drink, or another substance into the body.

lethargy: Lack of enthusiasm and energy; a common side effect of cannabis use.

Marihuana Tax Act of 1937: A marijuana taxation act that led to the prohibition of cannabis in the United States during much of the twentieth century.

marijuana: A cannabis plant that is smoked or consumed as a psychoactive (mind-altering) drug.

marijuana dispensary: A place where people can buy recreational or medical cannabis. Dispensaries are tightly controlled by the government.

marijuana oil: Liquid that is extracted from the hemp plant and placed in either capsule form or combined with foods or drinks. CBD is most commonly consumed as an oil.

medical cannabis identification card: A document issued by a state where it is legal to use medical cannabis; the card indicates that a patient may use, buy, or have medical cannabis at home, on his or her person, or both.

neuroprotectant: A substance that repairs and protects the nervous system, its cells, structure, and function.

neurotransmitter: Chemicals that communicate information in the human body.

opiates: Substances derived from the opium poppy plant such as heroin.

opium: A highly addictive narcotic drug that is created by collecting and drying the milky juice that comes from the seed pods of the poppy plant.

prohibition: The action of forbidding something, especially by law.

propaganda: False information that is created to influence people.

prosecution: The conducting of legal proceedings against someone if it is believed that they broke the law.

psychoactive drug: A drug that affects the mind.

psychosis: Detachment from reality.

receptors: Groups of specialized cells that can convert energy into electrical impulses.

repeal: To get rid of a law or congressional act.

shatter: Cannabis concentrate that looks like colored glass.

social cannabis use: The use of cannabis in social settings, whether in public or private.

tar: A toxic byproduct of cigarette or marijuana smoking.

tincture: A medicine made by dissolving a drug in alcohol, vinegar, or glycerites.

topicals: Cannabis-infused lotions, balms, and salves that relieve pain and aches at the application site on the body.

vaporizer: A device that is used to turn water or medicated liquid into a vapor for inhalation.

War on Drugs: An anti-drug campaign started in the United States in 1971 by then-president Richard Nixon. Its goal was to fight drug abuse and shipments of illegal drugs to the U.S. from Latin America, Mexico, and other places.

Index

activists, 56–57
addictions, 15, 17, 39, 41
adult-use cannabis, 72
alcohol, 65
American Journal of Public Health, 41
Amsterdam (Netherlands), 26–27, 63
anecdotal evidence, 18, 46, 55
anecdotal studies, 18–19
antioxidants, 9, 14
anxiety, 15–16, 35–36, 44
asthma, 17
Australia, 15

bad science, 68
bipolar disorder, 44
black markets, 20, 23, 39, 62
blind studies, 18, 36, 42
blood pressure, 18
Bortell, Alexis, 56
bronchitis, 18
Brookings Institution, 28

California City, 62
Canada, 7, 11, 24, 29, 40, 69
Canadian Medical Association Journal, 49
cancer, 15, 17, 29, 52, 57–58
cannabidiol (CBD), 11–12, 72
    benefits of, 13–14
cannabidiol oil, 8, 14, 66
cannabinoids, 11, 72
cannabis, 8
cannabis clubs, 72
cannabis products, 63
Cannabis sativa, 11
cannabis strains, 64, 72
CB2 receptors, 49
CBD oil, 57
Chinese medicine, 6
chronic obstructive pulmonary disease (COPD), 17
Cline, Dr. John, 37–38
clinical trials, 72
"coffee shops", 26–27
Colorado, 41, 64
controlled studies, 18, 22, 36, 42, 55, 67
Crohn's disease, 53

dabbing, 72
decriminalization, 24, 72
delta-9-tetrahydrocannabinol (THC), 72
    See also THC
Denmark, 25
depression, 13, 15, 33, 35–36, 38, 44
diabetes, 18, 29, 51
dispensaries, 20, 24, 73

dopamine, 72
Dravet's syndrome, 57
drug approvals, 54
drug overdoses, 41
drug-related deaths, 15, 40–41
drug trafficking, 72
drug treatment programs, 17

edibles, 11, 58, 72
education, 69–70
Egyptians, 6
electricity, 56
endocannabinoid system, 73
endocannabinoids, 32, 36
epilepsy, 14, 56
ethnocentrism, 21
euphoria, 73
extracts, 11, 73
eye drops, 51

fentanyl, 40
flashbacks, 34
Freud, Dr. Sigmund, 33
Fu Hsi, 6

genetics, 57
glaucoma, 6, 25, 27, 47, 50–51

hash, 73
heart attacks, 18
hemp, 10, 73
history, cannabis, 6
HIV/AIDS, 48–50
human body, 47
human trials, 60, 66

immune system, 46, 48
India, 6
industrial nations, 20
inflammation, 51–53
inflammatory bowel disorder, 50
insomnia, 37–40
Israel, 7, 24–25
    medical marijuana in, 21
    medical marijuana research in, 25, 29–30, 36, 53, 67

JAMA Internal Medicine, 15
Jamaica, 22–23
jobs, growth in, 62
Journal of Affective Disorders, 15
Journal of Psychoactive Drugs, 14

King's College (London), 36

lawmakers, 60–61
Leeuwenhoek's Disease, 54–55
legalization, 10, 64–65, 68–69
   Jamaica, 22
   process of, 61–65
   Uruguay, 23
lethargy, 73
lobotomies, 33–34
lung cancer, 17
lung-health, risks to, 17–18
lupus, 50

malnutrition, 46
Marihuana Tax Act (1937), 73
marijuana
   compared with tobacco, 17
   negative impacts of, 43
   overdoses, 43
   strains of, 64, 72
   understanding, 67–68
marijuana industry, 62
marijuana oil, 14, 66, 73
marijuana research, 25
Marinol, 25, 28
Mayo Clinic, 11
Medical Cannabis: Evidence on Efficacy, 55
medical marijuana, 7, 28, 52
   and addictions, 41
   benefits of, 13
   cancer, 15, 58
   Crohn's disease, 53
   Dravet's syndrome, 57
   and the elderly, 21
   and epilepsy, 14, 56
   future of, 61
   glaucoma, 25, 27, 47, 50–51
   and HIV/AIDS, 50
   and insomnia, 37–40, 50
   legalization of, 10
   lupus, 50
   migraines, 41
   Multiple Sclerosis, 14–15, 49
   opinions on, 6
   other countries, 22–23, 25
   post-traumatic stress disorder (PTSD), 14, 32, 34–35
   preparation of, 11
   rheumatoid arthritis, 53
   and teens, 14
   treating pain, 55
   uses, 9, 25
medical marijuana cards, 20, 22, 73
medical research, 14–15, 28–30, 37, 51
   barriers to, 66
   See also studies
medications, cannabis-derived, 25, 28

mental health
   and marijuana, 44
   science of, 33
mental illness, 33–34
mental impairment, 8
mental side effects, 12–13, 16
migraines, 48
minimum age for use, 24, 69
multiple sclerosis, 14–15, 29, 49
muscle spasms, 54
    See also multiple sclerosis

Nabilone, 25, 28
National Institute on Drug Abuse (NIDA), 12, 17
nausea, 9, 25, 28–30, 49–50, 52, 57–58
Netherlands, 7, 25–27
neurologists, 25
neuroprotectants, 73
Neurotoxicity Research, 36
neurotransmitters, 73
New England Journal of Medicine, 57

observational studies, 18–19
opiates, 73
opioid abuse crisis, 38–39, 41
opioids, 36
opium, 73
osteoarthritis, 30
overdoses, 40
   marijuana, 43
Oxycodone, 6, 10

pain, 9, 55
pain relief, 15, 30, 39, 55
paranoia, 16
penalties, 24, 27
personal responsibility, 60
placebos, 18, 22, 32, 36, 42, 49, 57
pneumonia, 18
post-traumatic stress disorder (PTSD), 14, 29, 32, 34–35, 44
prohibition, 74
propaganda, 74
prosecution, 74
psychoactive drugs, 8, 74
psychoactivity, 12–13
Psychology Today, 37–38
psychosis, 74
public opinions, 6, 9–10
   shaping, 21
public safety, concerns, 65

receptors, 74
recreational use, 20
   benefits of, 41
   legalization, 24, 64

relaxation, studies on, 42
rheumatoid arthritis, 53
Ritalin, 10, 69

Sativex, 14, 25, 28
Saudi Arabia, 27, 68
schedule I drugs, 8, 10, 30, 69
schedule II drugs, 10, 69
schizophrenia, 29, 32, 36, 44
seizures, 9, 55–56
shatter, 74
side effects, 7, 16–17, 46–47, 68
    insomnia, 38
    of overdoses, 43
    See also mental side effects
sleeping problems, 9
smoking, 11, 58, 68
spasticity, 14, 28
state laws vs. federal laws, 10, 64
statistics
    insomnia, 40
    marijuana use, 12
    overdoses, 41
    on studies, 67
stress, studies of, 36
stress-reduction, 15
studies, 28, 66–67
    Crohn's disease, 53
    Dravet's syndrome, 57
    duplicating, 67–68
    on insomnia, 38
    Israeli, 25, 29, 36, 53, 67
    Marijuana and PTSD, 29–30, 35
    on marijuana use, 9, 14–15, 17
    multiple sclerosis, 49
    pain relief, 55
    rheumatoid arthritis, 53
    types of, 18–19, 22, 36, 42

tar, 74
tax revenue, 60, 62, 64
teenagers, penalties for, 24
Tennessee, 61–62
tetrahydrocannabinol (THC), 8, 11–12
    See also THC
THC, 10, 14, 19, 29, 42, 51, 55–56, 67
    benefits, 13
    side effects, 12–13, 66
    See also tetrahydrocannabinol (THC)
tinctures, 74
tobacco, compared with marijuana, 17
topicals, 11, 68, 74
trauma, 44
    reliving, 16

United States, 69

Food & Drug Administration (FDA), 10, 54, 64
    government on marijuana, 10
    legalization, 10
    medical marijuana research, 30
    Veteran's Administration, 34
    War on Drugs, 26
Uruguay, 23–24, 28

vaping, 11, 58
vaporizers, 11, 74

War on Drugs, 26, 74
Washington Post (newspaper), 14
withdrawal symptoms, 17

Photo Credits

Cover: Peter Kim | Dreamstime.com

Cover: Katarzyna Bialasiewicz | Dreamstime.com

Title Page: Mario Cupkovic | Dreamstime.com

6–7: Hanohiki | Dreamstime

8: Olegmalyshev | Dreamstime

9: Olyina | Dreamstime

11: Vlad Ghiea | Dreamstime

13: Ocusfocus | Dreamstime

16: Katarzyna Bialasiewicz | Dreamstime

20: Nuvista | Dreamstime

21: Rafael Ben Ari | Dreamstime

26: Inna Felker | Dreamstime

27: Monkey Business Images | Dreamstime

31: Ongap | Dreamstime.com

32: Tracy King | Dreamstime

33: Monkey Business Images | Dreamstime

37: Rafael Ben Ari | Dreamstime

39: Stokkete | Dreamstime

40: Leszek Wrona | Dreamstime

43: Filip Kacalski | Dreamstime.com

45: Jeremynathan | Dreamstime.com

46: Atomazul | Dreamstime

47: Monkey Business Images | Dreamstime

48: Sebnem Ragiboglu | Dreamstime

52: Caleb Foster | Dreamstime

58: Sherry Young | Dreamstime.com

59: Dreamstime.com

60: Inginsh | Dreamstime

63: Thomas Lukassek | Dreamstime

65: Draghicich | Dreamstime

70–71: Eskymaks | Dreamstime.com

78

Further Reading & Internet Resources

Backes, Michael. *Cannabis Pharmacy: The Practical Guide to Medical Marijuana*. Revised ed. New York: Black Dog & Leventhal, 2017.

Blesching, Uwe. *The Cannabis Health Index: Combining the Science of Medical Marijuana with Mindfulness Techniques to Heal 100 Chronic Symptoms and Diseases*. Berkeley, Calif.: North Atlantic Books, 2015.

Hudak, John. *Marijuana: A Short History*. Washington, D.C.: Brookings Institution Press, 2016.

Lee, Martin A. *Smoke Signals: A Social History of Marijuana: Medical, Recreational and Scientific*. New York: Scribner, 2013.

Wolf, Laurie, and Mary Wolf. *The Medical Marijuana Dispensary: Understanding, Medicating, and Cooking with Cannabis*. New York: Althea Press, 2016.

Internet Resources

http://www.ncsl.org/research/health/state-medical-marijuana-laws.aspx This is the official website of the National Conference for State Legislatures. It provides information on current U.S. medical cannabis laws.

https://www.drugabuse.gov/drugs-abuse/marijuana This is the official U.S. government website for marijuana created by the National Institute on Drug Abuse (NIDA). It includes a description of marijuana and its health effects, as well as statistics and information on trends and research.

https://www.drugabuse.gov/publications/marijuana-facts-teens/want-to-know-more-some-faqs-about-marijuana This website from the NIDA answers frequently asked questions about marijuana such: How does marijuana work? Does marijuana use lead to other drugs? What happens if you smoke marijuana? What does marijuana do to the brain?

https://www.cdc.gov/marijuana/factsheets/teens.htm This website from the Centers for Disease Control and Prevention provides information on marijuana's effects on teens.

https://www.webmd.com/brain/ss/slideshow-medical-marijuana This website provides answers to frequently asked questions such as What Is medical marijuana? How does marijuana work on the brain? What are the short- and long-term side effects?

About the Author:

Leigh Clayborne is a health and wellness writer who lives in Nashville, Tennessee. She graduated from the University of Mississippi with a degree in education. She has worked in the medical industry for more than ten years and has written thousands of books and articles for others during her career. She speaks Spanish and volunteers as a English as a second language teacher. She is a micro-influencer on social media and maintains a regular blog that helps medical professionals better connect with patients through the internet.

Video Credits

Chapter 1:
Learn more about CBD and THC: http://x-qr.net/1EvP

Find out how countries like Australia are studying the benefits of medical marijuana on people who have cancer: http://x-qr.net/1HJ7

Chapter 2:
See how pharmacies in Uruguay screen people and distribute marijuana: http://x-qr.net/1Dg5

Learn more about marijuana research in Israel: http://x-qr.net/1Cqy

Chapter 3:
Learn more about the opioid crisis in the United States.: http://x-qr.net/1HkR

Learn more about how marijuana can impact those with bipolar disorder: http://x-qr.net/1DVB

Chapter 4:
Watch a video that shows how cannabis oil helped a little girl who was having seven-hundred seizures a day: http://x-qr.net/1EUG

Learn more about Alexis Bortell's struggle to gain access to a life-changing medicine to fight her seizures: http://x-qr.net/1Fdv

Chapter 5:
Find out how the marijuana industry is transforming the economy of the desert town of California City, California: http://x-qr.net/1HHE